MADE IN DAGENHAM

LEVEL 3

SCHOLASTIC

Adapted by: Paul Shipton

Publisher: Jacquie Bloese

Editor: Fiona Davis

Designer: Christine Cox

Picture research: Pupak Navabpour

Photo credits:
Pages 56 & 57: C Court/AFP, Keystone/Getty Images; Mirrorpix.
Pages 58 & 59: Evening Standard/Getty Images; Mirrorpix; Pictorial Press/Alamy.
Pages 60 & 61: Time Life Pictures, Bloomberg, L Jin/AFP/ Getty Images.

Published by Scholastic Ltd. 2011

Mary Glasgow Magazines (Scholastic Ltd.)
Euston House
24 Eversholt Street
London NW1 IDB

Printed in Singapore

Contents

MADE IN DAGENHAM

THE WORKERS

The workers are employed at the Ford factory in Dagenham in the UK. Most of the workers at the factory are men, but there are 187 women too. Many of the women are machinists. They use sewing machines to make car seat covers.

RITA
Rita is a young mother with two children. She is a machinist at the Ford factory.

CONNIE
Connie is the machinists' union representative. Her husband, George, is very ill.

EDDIE
Eddie is Rita's husband. He works at the factory too.

THE UNION

The union talks to the managers about any problems that the workers have.

ALBERT
Albert is the union representative for the Dagenham factory. He is popular with the workers.

MONTY TAYLOR
Monty works for the union head office.

THE MANAGEMENT

The managers work for the Ford Motor Company.

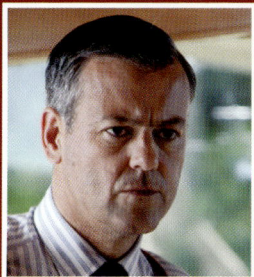

PETER HOPKINS
Hopkins is one of Ford's British managers. He is worried about all the strikes at the factory.

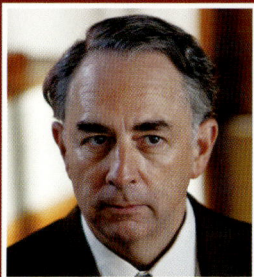

BOB TOOLEY
Tooley is Hopkins' boss in America. There are a lot of strikes at the Ford factories in the UK. He wants the strikes to stop.

LISA HOPKINS
Lisa is Peter's wife. Their son goes to the same school as Rita and Eddie's son.

THE GOVERNMENT

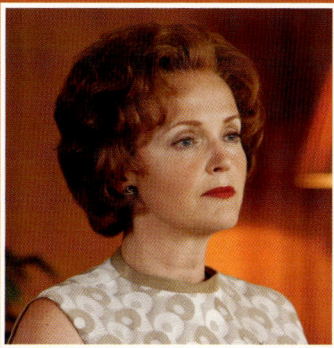

BARBARA CASTLE
Mrs Castle is an important politician. She is the new Employment Minister. It is her job to end all the strikes in the country.

❁ PLACES ❁

THE FORD MOTOR COMPANY
Ford is a huge car company from **Michigan** in the United States. In the 1960s Ford had several factories in the UK including the one at **Dagenham**, near London.

WESTMINSTER
This is the centre of the British government in London.

❁

This story takes place in **the UK** in **the 1960s**. This was a time when unions and the British government did not agree very much. At the end of the 1960s there were over 2,000 strikes in the UK.

The Ford Motor Company in *Made in Dagenham*

Head office management team, USA

Henry Ford II is the head of the company. A team manages the company. Bob Tooley is part of this team. Tooley and his team give instructions to the managers of the different factories.

Bob Tooley

The management, UK

A team of people manage each Ford factory. Peter Hopkins is the manager of the factory in Dagenham.

Peter Hopkins

The union

The union helps the workers. Albert and Connie are union representatives for the Dagenham factory. They tell the management about the women's complaints. Clive Bartholomew and Monty Taylor are the union leaders.

The union talks to the management.

Monty Taylor

The workers

Ford employs workers to make the cars. Rita, Eddie, Albert and Connie are all workers at the Dagenham factory.

The workers talk to the union.

Rita

Albert

The British Government

The British Government wants Ford to stay in Britain. The company provides thousands of jobs for British workers.

MADE IN DAGENHAM

In 1968 the Ford Motor Company produced 3,100 cars a day at its UK factories. Many of them were made at the huge factory in Dagenham. 55,000 men worked at the Dagenham factory ... and 187 women.

CHAPTER 1
The first vote

The Ford factory at Dagenham made cars, but none of the workers there came by car. The workers – and there were hundreds of them – just walked from the local estate or came by bicycle. Rita O'Grady and her husband Eddie always cycled together. They kissed goodbye at the factory gates.

'Bye, love. See you later.'

Eddie went to the main part of the factory and Rita cycled to the area where the machinists worked. Like Rita, most of the women machinists had husbands who worked for Ford too.

'Morning, Rita,' a young woman said.

'Morning, Sandra. Are you sure that skirt's short enough?' Rita joked.

Sandra was one of the youngest women at the factory. She was just twenty.

Inside, the radio was on as usual. 'It's the hottest day of the year,' the DJ was saying, 'so stay cool!'

The women didn't need a DJ to tell them that. It was terribly hot, and there weren't even any windows to let in fresh air. The women went to their work tables. They each had a table with a sewing machine. It was too hot to work in heavy work clothes. The women wore as few clothes as possible.

At eight o'clock exactly, the factory horn sounded. This was the start of the work day. The time for talk was over. Conversation was impossible over the sound of all the machines anyway. The women had to sew pieces of fabric together to make seat covers for the factory's cars. It was skilled work – it took thirteen different bits of fabric just to make one headrest for a seat. The women had to be quick, but they had to get it right, as well.

Rita looked up as her friend Connie hurried to the

machine next to hers. She was late again. This was happening more and more often these days.

'Everything all right?' Rita asked.

'Yes, I just woke up late.' Connie sat down at her machine and closed her eyes.

'How's George?' Rita could see the worry on her friend's face.

'Don't ask,' replied Connie. 'I've been awake half the night.' Connie's husband was very ill.

Suddenly some of the women shouted over the noise of the machines, 'Man!'

It was Albert, the union rep* for the factory. Many of the women quickly pulled extra clothes on.

'Cover yourselves up!' shouted Albert. 'What would your husbands say?'

The women laughed. Albert was the union rep because he really cared about the workers, and all the women loved him for it. If the workers in any part of the factory had a problem, they told Albert.

The women left their machines and came over. They were talking excitedly.

'Girls!' shouted Connie. She was the machinists' rep. 'This is important!'

The women continued to laugh and talk, until Albert shouted, 'Do you want to hear this or not?'

At last there was some quiet. 'In the words of Winston Churchill**,' began Albert importantly, 'this isn't the end. This …'

'Come on, Albert!' shouted one of the women. Her name was Brenda and she wasn't interested in important speeches or talk of famous politicians. Like all the women

* A union rep (representative) helps the workers who are in the union.

** Winston Churchill was the UK Prime Minister during World War II.

there, she wanted news from Albert. In the last few weeks, the company had said that they wanted to give the machinists a lower rate of pay. They had decided that the machinists' work was not skilled. The women told Albert and he had complained to the management. The women had even talked about having a one-day strike.

'The management still haven't replied to your complaint,' Albert told them.

Some of the women began talking again, angrily now.

'Sshhh!' said Rita. She wanted to hear Albert.

Albert continued. 'So now you all have to decide – are you going to stop all overtime, and have a one-day strike on May the 29th? Who votes yes?'

Everyone's hands went up.

Albert looked surprised. 'Anybody against?'

There were no hands in the air. Nobody had voted against the plan.

As they looked around, some of the women began to shout and laugh. They were excited and proud but also a little nervous. They had never done anything like this before.

'I'm seeing the management tomorrow,' Albert said with a proud smile. 'I'll tell them your decision.'

✿ ✿ ✿

The next day Rita got up first, as usual, and started to make breakfast for the family. Like most of the Ford workers, she and Eddie lived in a flat on the big housing estate near the factory. Rita had lived on the estate for her whole life.

She carried breakfast from the small kitchen to the table in the living room.

'Breakfast!' she shouted to her children. Sharon came quickly, but her older brother, Graham, was slow to come.

'I don't feel very well,' he said quietly when he finally appeared. He was eleven and in his first year at the grammar school*.

Rita knew when her son wasn't telling the truth. Then she saw them – red marks on one of his hands – and understood. One of the teachers had hit him … again.

'I didn't do anything,' Graham said quickly. 'Honestly.'

'Mr Clarke again?' Rita tried to hide her anger. 'It'll be fine,' she said. 'Eat your breakfast. I'll talk to him. OK?'

Before school started, Rita went to Graham's classroom. She knocked on the door.

'Yes,' answered a deep voice.

Rita felt nervous as she stepped inside. 'Can I have a word?'

---

* A grammar school is for students from eleven to eighteen years. You have to pass an exam to go there.

Mr Clarke was at the front of the class. 'Of course.' He was younger than Rita, but when he spoke to her, she felt like one of his students. 'How may I help?'

'You hit my son,' Rita said simply. 'On his hand … and it's not the first time.'

'And you are?'

'Mrs O'Grady.'

'Oh yes, O'Grady …' Mr Clarke said coolly. 'Yes, he forgot his books. And it's not the first time.'

'I don't care if it's the hundredth time,' said Rita, fighting to stay calm. 'I don't want you doing it.'

Mr Clarke looked at her for a moment. 'You come from the estate, don't you?'

'I don't see why that …'

Mr Clarke spoke over her. 'Boys from the estate often find it difficult at grammar school,' he said. 'It isn't really their fault. Their parents are not able to help them.' He smiled. 'But the boys learn in time. And your son will too … if you just give him the chance.'

Before Rita could even think of how to reply, Mr Clarke said, 'Thank you for your time, Mrs O'Grady.' He turned away. The meeting was over.

Outside the classroom, Rita ran for the school door with hot tears in her eyes. People like Mr Clarke were never going to change their opinions about boys from the estate, or about men and women who worked at the factory. But most of all, Rita was angry with herself. She had come here to fight for her son, but instead she had been unable to find any words.

Another mother was walking towards her. She was tall and blonde and was wearing expensive clothes. She looked at Rita and asked, 'Are you OK?'

It was clear from her voice and her clothes that she didn't live on the estate or work at the factory. Rita pushed past her without a word.

CHAPTER 2
'Everybody out!'

'Here it comes!' cried one of the women.

At the first sound of rain, the machinists had to move quickly. If they didn't, the rain would come into the work area. Connie kept an umbrella near her sewing machine. She was putting this up over her work table when Albert appeared in front of her. He clearly had important news.

'There's a meeting tomorrow at the Ford head office in Warley,' he told her excitedly. Other women left their machines to listen too, so he spoke louder. 'The managers couldn't *believe* that you were talking about a strike!'

The women cheered. The company was listening to them now.

'There'll be three managers there.' Albert started to count. 'Who will we have? There's Monty Taylor from the union head office … me … Connie … We need one more.'

'Why?' asked Eileen. She was one of the older machinists. In all her time at Ford, she had never seen anything like this.

'It's a little trick that I learned in the war*,' Albert smiled. 'Always arrive with more people than they have! So … who's going to be our fourth man?'

Nobody answered. Several women shook their heads.

Albert tried again. 'Come on – it's a day off work!'

That changed things! Immediately most of the women put their hands up.

'Oh, so you all want to go now!' said Albert. 'Well …' He stopped as his eyes met Rita's. Her arms were crossed and she was listening to everything carefully.

* When people in the UK say 'the war', they usually mean World War II (1939–45).

Albert just looked at her.

'What?' asked Rita.

The rest of the women understood and they knew that Rita was a good choice.

'You should do it,' a few women said to her. Connie nodded in agreement.

Rita didn't say anything for a few seconds. This wasn't the sort of thing that she usually did. But a day away from the factory sounded OK, and it was a chance to speak for the machinists for once …

She smiled. 'Go on then.'

✿ ✿ ✿

The next day Rita and Connie went with Albert and Monty Taylor to the meeting at the Ford head office. Monty was older than Albert. He was a big man with grey hair and a grey moustache. He worked for the union. Meetings with management were just part of his job.

On the way to the Ford head office, Monty said, 'We've got time for lunch before the meeting.'

Rita looked at the restaurant nervously. It looked expensive to her. She was wearing her best dress, but was it nice enough for a place like this?

'Monty always comes here,' whispered Connie.

During lunch Monty explained how he wanted the meeting to be. He had had a lot of meetings with the managers from Ford and he knew the best way of talking to them.

'Here's a little advice,' he told Rita. 'If they ask you a question, I'll answer it for you. If I nod, you nod. OK?'

'Right,' said Rita nervously.

❀ ❀ ❀

At the meeting, the three managers – all of them men – sat on one side of the table. Monty, Albert, Rita and Connie sat on the other side. The two women followed Monty's instructions and stayed quiet.

'The women at the Dagenham factory are still waiting for a reply to their complaint,' Albert began. 'That's why we're sitting here now. They believe that their work is skilled.'

'I understand what the girls are saying …' began one of the managers. This was Peter Hopkins and he seemed to be the boss.

Monty Taylor held up a hand. 'Please don't speak for the girls, Mr Hopkins,' he said with a smile. 'None of us knows what's in a woman's head!'

Rita sat in silence but she was becoming angrier and angrier. Monty didn't want Hopkins to speak for 'the girls', but he was happy to speak for them himself.

Hopkins continued. 'The machinists are not the only

workers here at Ford who have questions to discuss with management. They must wait their turn.'

Monty's smile became friendlier. 'Look, you know me,' he said. 'I haven't got any problems with Ford. Let's agree to meet again in two weeks' time. We'll come back and at that time you can listen to the girls' complaint. If we do that, you can tell your bosses that you stopped the strike because of today's meeting. And we can go back to the girls and tell them that you'll listen to their complaints in a few weeks' time.'

'That seems fair,' said Hopkins.

'I'm not sure that the girls will see it that way,' said Albert crossly.

'The girls will be fine,' Monty told him. 'They'll know that the union – not management – is making decisions for them. That's what matters to the girls.'

'Rubbish!'

It was Rita who said this. She had listened and listened, but she couldn't stay silent any longer. 'I'm sorry, but it *is* rubbish.' She looked straight at Monty. 'What do you know about what matters to the girls?'

Rita pulled some pieces of fabric out of her handbag. She threw them on the table. 'There! Put them together. Go on!'

'You stole those,' said one of the managers. 'They belong to the Ford Company.'

'Oh, stop it,' Rita told him. She pointed to the bits of fabric. 'We have to take all these different pieces and make a car seat cover. There aren't any instructions. That is *skilled* work.' She shook her head. 'You need to take an exam to do our work!'

Hopkins spoke over her. 'Please, Miss …'

'It's *Mrs* O'Grady.'

'Mrs O'Grady, I understand why you are unhappy, but …'

'No, you don't understand,' said Rita, 'but it's not difficult. Our work is skilled and we should get the pay for that.'

'Mrs O'Grady …' Hopkins tried again, but Rita stopped him.

'I haven't finished … You're saying that we have to wait our turn, but we made our complaint *months* ago! You've just done nothing about it. And we all know why – when the men at the factory go on strike, the management has to listen to them. But the women have never been on strike before, have we? You thought that we'd all just go away. Well, I'm sorry we're not going anywhere.' She looked right at Hopkins, no longer nervous. 'We're going to do what we said: no more overtime,' Rita thought for a moment, 'and an *immediate* twenty-four hour strike. After that, well, that's up to you.' She stood up. 'Excuse me – we have to go now.'

As Rita walked away, the men at the table didn't know what to say. Only Albert had a proud smile on his face.

Outside the building he was still smiling. But not Monty. He was really angry. 'Do you think I like looking stupid in front of Hopkins?' he shouted at Albert. Then he just walked off and left them.

Albert didn't care. 'I knew you were right for this job,' he told Rita. He waved the pieces of fabric. 'It was a brilliant idea to bring these.'

'Oh no, I didn't bring them for the meeting.' Rita shook her head. 'That manager was right – I was stealing them. Eddie mends the tent with them when we go on holiday.' She held out her hand. 'Can I have them back, please?'

❀ ❀ ❀

It was late afternoon when Rita and Connie returned to the factory. The sewing area was busy, filled with the usual sound of sewing machines.

'What are we going to say?' Rita asked her friend.

'You tell them,' answered Connie. 'You're the one who made this happen.'

The noise of the sewing machines stopped when the machinists noticed the two women. Everybody wanted to hear what had happened.

Rita climbed onto a chair. She looked around at all the faces there. She worked every day with these women. They were her friends. She smiled nervously.

'Everybody out!' she said.

The women had talked about this moment, but it was still a surprise to hear the words. There was a nervous, excited feeling in the air. Several women kissed Rita and Connie on their way to the door. The women of Dagenham were going on strike!

CHAPTER 3
The right woman for the job

The next morning at the factory was very different from usual. The women workers met outside the factory gates. A few of them were writing signs. One said: 'FAIR PAY FOR A FAIR DAY'S WORK'.

The women talked excitedly. Sandra was showing her new eye make-up to some of the women.

'This is a strike, not a party!' joked one of the older women.

The sun was shining, and it almost felt like a party. The men were still going to work as usual, but a lot of them shouted their support for the women.

Eddie stopped on his bike and gave Rita a quick kiss. 'Good luck,' he told her.

When everyone was ready, Rita and Connie closed the metal gates to the machinists' area. Now no trucks could come in or out.

'Now they'll know that we're serious,' Rita smiled.

The women took their places in front of the gate. Rita and Connie were right in the middle. They held their signs proudly in the air. This was their first strike and they were ready for anything …

Nothing happened. Minutes passed and still nothing happened. Work continued as usual in the rest of the factory. No trucks tried to pass through the gates.

'Would anyone like a cup of tea?' said Brenda at last.

'Yes!'

'Good idea!'

Most of the women put down their signs and went off for a hot drink. Only Connie and Rita stayed in front of the gate. They put their sign down on the ground.

'It's heavy, isn't it?' said Rita.

❀ ❀ ❀

Manager Peter Hopkins didn't want to make the phone call. But he knew that it couldn't wait any longer.

'Get me Tooley,' he said into the phone.

A few moments later an American voice was at the other end of the phone.

'What is it?' It was Bob Tooley, one of the managers at Ford's main office in the United States.

'We've got a problem with the workers here, I'm afraid,' said Hopkins.

'Another one?' said the American. 'Who is it this week?'

Hopkins hated making these calls. He knew that Tooley was angry. 'It's the women,' Hopkins said.

❀ ❀ ❀

By late afternoon it had begun to rain again. Some of the women pulled coats up over their heads. Others ran to find somewhere dry near the factory gate. Rita looked up at the dark skies. What should they do now?

'We've done a full day,' she said, 'and we've got our message across.' She smiled. 'OK then … we've finished for today! Everyone go home!'

As the women started to leave, Brenda turned to Rita.

'Hey, Rita,' she said. 'Well done!'

Rita looked unsure.

'We couldn't have done this without you, could we?' shouted Brenda as she ran out into the rain.

❀ ❀ ❀

It was still raining when Rita hurried through the centre of town. She was carrying several signs and she was completely wet.

As she passed a little café, somebody inside knocked on the window. It was Albert. He pointed at the café door. He wanted to tell her something.

'Can I have a word?'

'I can't, Albert,' Rita began. 'I have to get Graham from school and …'

Albert took her by the arm and smiled. 'I'll get you a cup of tea,' he said.

'Go on then … just for a few minutes.'

When they were at the table, Albert gave Rita a serious look. He spoke carefully. He had thought about this a lot.

'This problem isn't about skilled or unskilled work,' he began. 'Ford decided to give you less money because they *can*. They can pay women less money than men. All over the country, Rita, women are getting less, because they're *women*. You'll always come second until …'

'Until we get equal pay,' said Rita. 'I understand.' She looked at Albert. 'But there's something that I don't understand. Why is it so important to you, Albert?'

Albert was quiet for a moment.

'My dad didn't live with us,' he said slowly. 'My mum worked hard all her life to give everything to me and my brothers. And she earned less than half of what the men in the factory got … for the same work. Nobody thought that it could ever be different. Companies have done this for years and somebody has got to stop them.' He looked into Rita's eyes. '*You* can change things. You *can*, Rita – believe me.'

Rita shook her head uncertainly. 'What about Connie? She's our rep, we voted for her.'

Albert continued to look right at her. 'This needs a leader. It needs someone to explain all the points clearly. Connie can't do that, not at the moment …'

Rita nodded. It was true. Connie had too much to do already – after a full day at work, she had to care for her husband, George, at home.

'Don't say anything now,' continued Albert. 'Just think about it, will you?'

Rita didn't reply. Albert believed that she was the right woman for the job. But did *she* believe it?

✿ ✿ ✿

The rain was falling even harder when Rita arrived at Graham's school. She had no umbrella.

'Do you want to wait in here?' shouted a woman's voice from a car by the side of the road.

Rita shook her head. 'I'll make everything wet.'

But the woman pushed the passenger door open.

'Come on, quick!'

As Rita got into the car, she looked down at all the drops of water from her hair. 'I'm sorry,' she said.

'It doesn't matter,' the blonde woman said. 'We've met before – in the school a couple of days ago. Do you remember?'

Rita nodded, feeling bad at the thought. She had pushed past this woman after her meeting with Graham's teacher. She looked now at the blonde woman's expensive earrings and beautiful red dress. Rita loved the dress. She had seen it in a fashion magazine. She knew that she would never have the money to buy a dress like it.

The blonde woman smiled. 'I wanted to see you again,' she told Rita. 'I wanted to ask if you would sign a letter. I've complained to the head teacher about Mr Clarke.'

'You mean … you went to see Mr Clarke too?'

The woman nodded. 'He hit my son in class. But when I complained, Mr Clarke didn't listen to a word. You can't talk to him.'

Rita nodded. They were from different worlds, but they were both mothers who just wanted to protect their sons.

'OK,' she said with a smile. 'Give me a pen. I'll sign your letter too.'

CHAPTER 4
'Equal pay or nothing!'

Brian spent most of the working day cleaning different parts of the Dagenham factory. Sometimes he had to carry messages. He didn't mind this job, but there was one place that he didn't like going to – the machinists' area. As soon as he stepped into the work area, the shouts began.

'Man!'

A few machinists began to laugh and cheer. 'Cover yourselves up, girls!'

Brian tried not to look as he walked towards Connie's machine. He pulled a pile of letters from his pocket and handed them to her. There was one for each of the machinists. As Connie passed them out, nobody laughed and joked anymore – this was serious. It was a letter from the management about the strike.

Rita opened the letter and read. With every sentence, she became angrier. Why had the management sent them a letter like this?

✿ ✿ ✿

A couple of hours later, Monty Taylor was at the factory. He came as soon as Albert told him about the letter from the management.

Albert and the women waited as Monty read the letter. Monty looked up. 'Just forget about it,' he said.

'Forget about it?' asked Rita uncertainly. 'It says that we "chose to break the company's rules".'

'That's what they *always* say on the day after a strike,' Monty explained calmly. 'They don't mean it.'

'So why are they saying it then?'

Monty was becoming impatient. 'Because that is how

we've *always* done it, in every strike. Those are the rules.'

But Rita didn't want to hear one of Monty's little speeches. 'No, sorry, we aren't playing that game. We aren't your *men*, remember? We're *us*. And we won't be spoken to like this.' Rita waved the letter in the air. 'I'm calling for more strike action,' she continued, 'until we get the same rates of pay as the men.'

'What?' asked Monty sharply. There were sounds of surprise all around the room. Nobody had said anything about equal pay before.

'That's what this is really about, isn't it?' Rita said to Monty. 'We do skilled work but we're on the lowest rate in the factory. There's only one possible reason. It's because we're women.'

She was speaking louder now, looking around the room. The other women were nodding in agreement. Rita was saying what they all knew to be the truth.

'Women always get paid less. We have to demand a fair rate of pay. It should depend on the skill of the work, not the sex of the worker!'

The women were laughing now, cheering in agreement at Rita's words. Albert just stood quietly and listened.

'This strike is about just one thing,' continued Rita. 'Fairness. Equal pay or nothing! Who votes yes to further strike action? No work until we get fair pay!'

Every woman in the room put her hand in the air.

Rita smiled. 'Everybody out!' she shouted.

As the women started to leave, Monty gave Albert a dark look.

'What?' asked Albert. 'I didn't make them do it.' But he couldn't hide the smile on his face.

✿ ✿ ✿

Monty was back at the union head office with his boss, Bartholomew. It was clear that Bartholomew wasn't very happy about the news from Dagenham.

'Equal pay for women?' said Bartholomew. 'What were you thinking, Monty?' Bartholomew believed in workers' rights. But he had an important job at the union and this was going to be difficult for him.

'It wasn't me!' cried Monty. 'It was Albert's fault! He spoke to the women when I wasn't there ...'

'Get him in here,' said Bartholomew.

Monty hurried out to where Albert sat alone in a waiting room. 'I tried to protect you, Albert,' Monty lied, 'but you are in big trouble.'

Silently Albert followed him back inside the office.

'This is difficult, Albert,' began Bartholomew. 'The unions are in talks with management about a lot of things. This problem with the Dagenham women puts all of those talks in danger. We understand, of course, but we have to remember who comes first. Karl Marx* himself said, "Men make their own history." That's MEN, Albert!'

Albert replied, 'Didn't Marx also say that a woman's position in society is a sign of progress? Or was that a different Karl Marx? Equal pay – we should fight for that, and you know it.' He looked from Bartholomew to Monty. 'Isn't it the union's job to support its workers? This girl Rita is braver than both of you. I am going to help her. And you should do the same.'

❁ ❁ ❁

The strike was very different this time. It wasn't just a single day with no work. Now the women refused to go

* Karl Marx (1818–83) was a German writer and thinker. Some of his political ideas led to the start of the unions.

back to work until they got what they wanted. Every day there was a line of strikers outside the factory gate. Trucks were turned away.

At first the strike was reported in just the local newspapers. But Rita did everything that she could to explain the workers' fight to people outside the factory.

Every time Rita stood up and gave a speech, she became more confident. By the time a group of the Dagenham women travelled by bus to the Ford factory near Liverpool*, she was no longer nervous in front of large crowds. The Liverpool machinists listened carefully to her message.

* Liverpool is a big city in the North West of England.

'You do the same job for Ford here in Liverpool that we do in Dagenham,' she told them. 'You know that we do skilled work. I'm asking you to strike now, not just for machinists like us … but for *all* women. I'm asking you to strike for what is right. And that means the same pay as men. If you want to join us, put your hands in the air now!'

There was a great cheer as the Liverpool machinists' hands went up.

It was a long drive back to Dagenham from Liverpool. When she arrived home, Rita was tired but happy with the day's work.

Eddie was still in the kitchen, washing the dishes. 'How was it?' he asked.

'It was amazing, Eddie. Every one of them voted to join us. We're going to be in the national newspapers tomorrow.'

Eddie nodded. 'Well done,' he said quietly.

Rita went to the stairs. 'I'll kiss the kids goodnight.'

Eddie said nothing. He had burned the family's dinner again that night, and there were still dishes to wash. He didn't have any clean shirts ready for work in the morning. He loved Rita and he wanted to support her fight. But he wasn't sure that he was happy with how his life had changed.

CHAPTER 5
No more jobs

Barbara Castle was working in her offices at Westminster. She was one of the top politicians in the government. As the country's new Employment Minister* – the first woman to have the job – she had one of the most difficult jobs in the government. This meant trying to do something about all the strikes. In the last two years there had been more strikes than at any other time in the country's history. It had cost the UK millions of pounds.

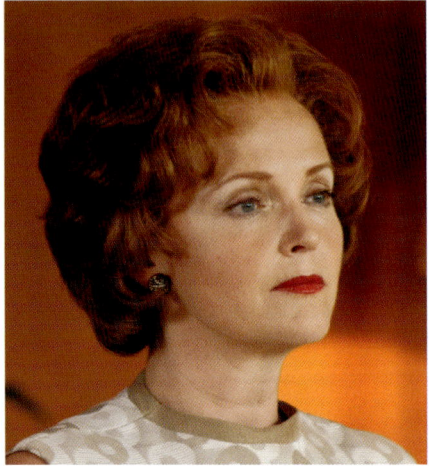

She looked up from her desk now. It was hard to work because of all the noise from outside today – car horns and shouts. Something was happening outside. She went to the window and saw why. There was a group of women on the grass outside the building. As soon as she saw the signs about equal pay, Mrs Castle understood. These were the Dagenham women. She had followed their fight with the Ford management carefully in the news.

She read the biggest of the signs over the women's heads. It said:

'WE WANT SEX.'

* A Minister is one of the top positions for politicians in the British government.

Down on the grass, Rita and Connie were surprised at all the support from everyone around them. People were shouting out as they drove past.

'I finish work at four!' called one man from a white van.

Rita looked up at the big sign and understood.

'Girls!' she said quickly. 'People can't see all of the words on the sign!'

Brenda and Sandra laughed and opened up the sign fully. Moments later, people could read what it said:

'WE WANT SEX EQUALITY.'

Back in Dagenham, Eddie was having a quick drink after work at the factory bar with his friend, Dave. They both looked up at the black-and-white pictures on the television. Rita was on the news! She was still in London.

A reporter was asking her about the strike. 'How long are you ready to stay out?'

'As long as it takes,' replied Rita.

'Does your husband support you?'

'He has to!' shouted Brenda over Rita's shoulder. While the others were laughing, Rita added, 'Of course he supports us. We supported the men when they were out on strike.'

Back in Dagenham, Dave pointed at the TV. 'Can you believe that? You must be proud of her.'

Eddie nodded uncomfortably. 'Yes, she's … doing OK.' He stood up. 'I've got to go.'

'Already?'

'Rita won't be home until late,' Eddie said. 'I've got to feed the kids.'

On the way out he put his glass on the bar. Connie's husband, George, was sitting there. He often came and drank in the club, but never with friends. George always drank alone.

'You tell her to end this now,' he said to Eddie with a dark look. 'This strike has gone on long enough.'

'They don't want it to continue, George,' replied Eddie.

'It's OK for you. I can't work. We've got no money,' George said.

'I know that,' said Eddie softly. George hadn't been able to work for a long time now. Eddie wasn't sure what the problem was exactly, but it had started after the war. People said that George had fought bravely in the war, but it had changed him.

'They're going to reach an agreement,' Eddie continued.

George said nothing. He just went back to his private thoughts.

✿ ✿ ✿

Rita was walking home from the shops. She was surprised to see lots of men from the factory. They were cycling home.

'You're a bit early,' she said to a few of the men. 'What's happening?'

One of the men stopped his bike in front of Rita. 'They can't make cars without car seats,' he said angrily, 'and there are no more car seats because of your strike. No more seats, no more jobs … for any of us. Ford has sent everybody home without pay. They've shut the factory and it's *your* fault. Well done!'

As more and more bikes passed her, Rita knew that everything had changed now. She started to run home. She had to see Eddie.

✿ ✿ ✿

At the main offices of Ford in Michigan, USA, Tooley was looking at a photo of Rita O'Grady in the newspaper. This was the woman who was making so much trouble for the company.

'Who *is* this woman?' shouted a voice from the speaker-phone on the desk. It was Tooley's boss, Henry Ford II himself. He was the head of the whole company. 'What do we know about her? Who's she with?'

'We don't think that she's with any group,' said Tooley. 'She hasn't got any political history, either in or out of the union. She just has a problem with Ford.'

'A problem!' shouted Ford. 'We'll *all* have a problem if she gets what she wants. We'll have to give equal pay *right across the world*! Do you understand that, Tooley?'

'Yes, sir, I do.'

'Good! So get on the next flight to England. I want this strike to stop!'

❀ ❀ ❀

When Rita came back home, Eddie was sitting in bed with a book.

'Are you OK?' she asked.

'Yeah.' Eddie didn't even look up. 'Been busy, have you?' he asked.

Rita sat on the bed. She knew from his voice that something was wrong. 'Listen, Eddie … we're almost at the end. Ford are losing too much money with the whole factory shut. I'm sorry about you and the boys at the factory, but …'

'Don't worry about us, Rita!' Eddie said. His voice was hard. 'At least it's nice warm weather. It won't be so bad if we can't pay to heat the flat.' He gave her a quick, cool smile.

Rita sat at the mirror and started to get ready for bed. 'The thing is, Eddie, I know how you feel. I remember all those times when the men went on strike. And the women all supported you then. That meant no work for us.'

'Yeah.' Eddie went back to his book.

Rita was becoming angry now. 'Listen, Eddie, if there's something you want to say to me …'

'There's nothing.'

'Good. It hasn't been the easiest day for me either.'

But Eddie wasn't listening. He had put down his book and turned off the light.

❀ ❀ ❀

Peter Hopkins was nervous. Until today, Bob Tooley had been no more than a voice on the telephone. Now he was here in England.

Hopkins had collected the American from the airport and invited him to dinner at his house.

'Come in,' Hopkins said. 'My wife's cooking dinner.'

Tooley shook Lisa Hopkins' hand. 'I was telling Peter that I'm happy to eat later at the hotel.'

'It's no trouble,' said Lisa.

Hopkins wanted to please his boss. 'She loves to cook,' he said brightly.

After dinner, Hopkins sat back as his wife began to take plates from the table.

'Lisa?' said Tooley. 'Peter tells me that you studied history at Cambridge University.'

'Yes,' Lisa smiled, 'I did.'

Tooley continued. 'What do you think about our little problem at the factory? Maybe your husband isn't being hard enough with the strikers?'

'No, not at all!' answered Lisa. 'Look at the other car companies in the country. They don't have problems with the unions. I think it's because their style of management allows more discussion.' She put the plates down. 'But at Ford, you only talk to the unions because you have to.'

Hopkins looked nervously from his wife to his boss. Tooley was smiling politely. He clearly hadn't expected this kind of answer.

'That's an interesting opinion,' he said, looking at Peter, 'don't you think?'

Hopkins didn't know what to say. He didn't want his boss to think that his wife supported the unions in any way. At last he thought of something.

'Cheese!' he said to Lisa. 'Why don't you get the cheese?'

CHAPTER 6
Life on strike

During the long days on strike, the women spent a lot of time together. Several of them were at Brenda's house when Rita arrived with their strike pay. She handed it to each woman in a little brown envelope.

'Is that all?' asked Sandra when she saw the money from the union. It was just three pounds.

'You don't have to take it,' Rita told her.

'No, it's OK, I'll have it!' replied Sandra.

It was even harder for the women with husbands and children – three pounds wasn't much to feed the family and pay the bills for the week.

Brenda didn't have to worry about food. She didn't have to worry about fruit and vegetables anyway – her boyfriend had a shop. She gave fruit and vegetables to the other women too.

Rita didn't stay at Brenda's for long. She had to give the strike pay to all the other women. The first house she went to was Connie's. When Rita arrived, her friend was getting some potatoes ready for dinner.

'Albert called me,' Rita told her. 'There's a meeting at the union. He thinks that we both should go.'

Connie didn't look up. 'No, I don't think so.'

'What are you talking about?'

'George is ill, Rita. You know that.' There was a frightened look in Connie's eyes. 'And this strike is making him worse – much worse. I've got to look after George. He only has me.'

'You've got a life too,' Rita told her friend softly. 'You've got to live it. Or the war's going to destroy two people …'

✿ ✿ ✿

'Monty, this is Mr Tooley,' said Peter Hopkins at the Ford offices in Warley.

Tooley already knew about Monty Taylor and he wasn't interested in long conversations. 'Good afternoon, Mr Taylor,' the American said simply. 'Go and break this strike, please.'

For Monty this was just another part of the same old game between union and management. 'I don't think you understand whose side I'm on,' he began.

'Yes, I do,' said Tooley calmly. 'I've read all about you.' He opened some notes on the desk in front of him. 'You seem to be on *your* side, Mr Taylor.'

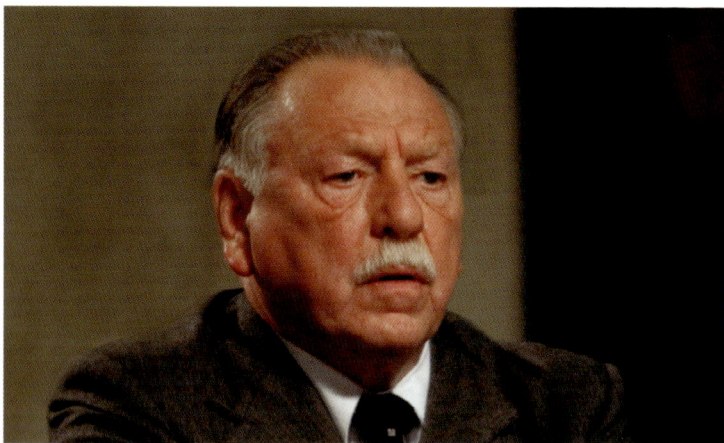

Monty wasn't expecting this. He stood up, ready to leave. 'I don't have to listen to this,' he told Hopkins.

'Keep walking,' said Tooley, 'and in six months, your union won't exist.'

Monty stopped.

'Our company does not have the money to pay women the same as men,' continued Tooley. 'That is a fact. If it has to, Ford will not survive. And with no workers to give them money, the unions will disappear. That means you too, Mr Taylor.'

He looked back at the papers on the desk. On the top page there was a list of all the restaurants where Monty had eaten lunch on his way to union meetings. 'That means no more nice lunches that the unions pay for. No more free trips to union conferences.' He stepped closer to Monty. 'If these women get what they want, *you* are in big trouble. So … go and break the strike, Mr Taylor. As soon as possible.'

Monty left the room in silence.

✿ ✿ ✿

When Rita got home, two men were carrying a fridge down the stairs of her building.

'That's our fridge! ' she said. 'What's happening?'

The men didn't stop. Eddie was watching them from the stairs.

'We didn't finish paying for it,' he told Rita angrily. 'So they're taking it away!'

'Why didn't you use the money in the kitchen cupboard?' asked Rita.

'Because I had to pay the milkman*,' shouted Eddie. 'But now we haven't got a fridge to put the milk in!'

'Why didn't you tell him that you'd pay next week?' cried Rita, following him back up the stairs. Now she was shouting too.

Eddie turned outside the door to their flat. 'Welcome to the real world, Rita,' he said coldly. 'This is life when you're on strike. You've got no money and you start screaming at your partner.'

✿ ✿ ✿

* A milkman brings milk to people's houses every morning.

Connie was getting ready for the meeting at the union offices. George just stood and watched.

'You're going, are you?' he said.

Connie couldn't look him in the eyes. 'You know I'm going. I told you.' She stopped at the door. 'Rita asked me. You've got to fight for what you believe in … You know that, George.' Connie smiled. She remembered the man that George had been in the past. He had fought for his beliefs in the war.

'Do you think I'd do the same if there was another war?' he asked.

'I know you would,' she said proudly.

George's eyes didn't move from Connie's face. 'I love you,' he told her, and for once he sounded stronger – almost like the old George.

Connie moved towards him, but George just smiled bravely. 'Go,' he told her.

✿ ✿ ✿

Albert was waiting for Rita and Connie at the union building. As soon as they arrived, a secretary said, 'Mr Bartholomew will see you now.'

As they went into the union leader's office, Albert spoke quickly and quietly. 'The strike is becoming a problem for the union now. So don't believe anything that Bartholomew tells you, OK?'

Inside the office, Monty Taylor was sitting with Bartholomew.

'This union is still supporting you and the girls, Rita,' Bartholomew began, 'but … we think that it's time to discuss this important question with the other unions. They can vote on it at Eastbourne.'

Rita understood. Every year representatives from all the different unions met at a big conference. This year it was in a hotel in the seaside town of Eastbourne.

Bartholomew continued. 'If the other unions in the country vote to support you – and we *expect* them to support you – then the strike can continue until you get what you want.'

Monty smiled at the women. 'But of course, the vote at Eastbourne will be final. We'll have to follow any decision that they make.'

❀ ❀ ❀

'I don't believe a word that Monty Taylor says,' laughed Connie as they walked home after the meeting. 'He just wants the strike to end.'

'And he wants the other unions to end it for him,' agreed Rita. 'We'll just have to go to Eastbourne and speak to the conference before he does,' she added bravely.

Connie went up the path to her house. 'See you tomorrow, Rita.'

'Monty Taylor's not going to win!' Rita called after her with a smile. 'We are!'

She walked on towards her flat. But then she heard a terrible scream from behind her. It had come from Connie's house.

Rita ran back to the house as fast as she could. She found her friend at the door to the living room.

George's body was hanging from the light with a belt around his neck. He was dead.

❀ ❀ ❀

A lot of Ford workers were at George's funeral. Rita stood with Eddie and the children under the dark sky. Connie stood at her husband's grave and held Brenda's hand. She looked pale and tired.

As Connie started to leave the church, Rita hurried to her. This was the first time that she had seen her friend since George's death.

'I'm so sorry, Connie,' Rita said.

'No, you're not.' Connie was upset. 'I wasn't there for him. He needed me.'

'That's enough, Connie,' said Brenda. She led her away.

Eddie was by Rita's side. He took her hand, but the tears were already falling down her face.

CHAPTER 7
Eastbourne

Later that day, Rita was alone in the flat. She didn't know what to think. Did it really matter if she went to Eastbourne or not? Her friend's husband was dead. The strike seemed unimportant now.

Suddenly there was a knock on the door. She opened it and looked into the face of Lisa Hopkins.

'This is a surprise,' said Rita. There were still tears in her eyes. 'Listen, it isn't really a good time.' She didn't want to speak to anybody. And she really didn't want to speak to someone who didn't know anything about life on the estate or work at the factory.

Lisa nodded quickly. She seemed uncomfortable too. 'I just wanted to tell you … the school has asked Mr Clarke to leave.' She gave a nervous smile. 'We won!'

Suddenly Rita remembered Mr Clarke. 'That's great!' she said.

Lisa turned to leave, but then stopped. 'I'm married to Peter Hopkins,' she said.

It took Rita a moment to understand. 'What?'

'I thought that perhaps you didn't know.'

'I don't understand but …' Rita was beginning to feel angry. 'I wasn't joking. I've had a terrible day. If you've come to ask me to end the strike, then …'

'No!' said Lisa quickly. She took Rita's hand. 'Keep going. *Please* keep going! Do you know who I am? Who I *really* am?'

Rita shook her head.

'I'm Lisa Burnett. I'm thirty-one years old. I studied history at one of the best universities in the world, but my husband likes to think that I'm stupid.' Tears were coming to her eyes now. 'When I was studying, I was very, very happy. I loved reading about all these amazing people making history. And I just wondered what it felt like. So let me know, will you? When *you've* finished making history?' She smiled at Rita. 'Don't stop the fight.'

✿ ✿ ✿

'Rita, where are you going?' Eddie jumped up. Rita was wearing her best dress and walking to the door. He ran out of the flat after her.

She was already on the stairs. 'Eastbourne,' she answered without stopping.

Eddie didn't understand. 'I thought that you decided not to go!' he cried, following her down the stairs.

'I've *got* to go.'

He caught her outside the building. 'Rita, stop! We … we've got to talk. I know that it hasn't been good between us. But …'

'Eddie, I've got to get on the bus …' began Rita.

'No, just listen to me!' It was hard for him to find the words. 'If I haven't supported you enough, then I'm sorry. But you haven't been perfect in all of this either.'

'The girls are waiting for me.' Rita turned to go. 'This isn't the time, Eddie.'

'Yes, it is!' cried Eddie. 'You think that I don't care enough. That I'm more interested in working on my motorbike or something like that. But I try my best. I don't go out to the pub every night. I've never thought about other women. In all our years together, I've never hit you … or the kids.'

Now Rita was upset. 'Oh, lucky me!' she said. 'So you're perfect because you don't hit us? But that's how it should be! Don't you understand, Eddie? That is how it should be! This is what this strike is all about.'

She turned and walked away, leaving Eddie alone with his thoughts.

✿ ✿ ✿

At the hotel in Eastbourne the conference had already started. A few hundred union reps – all men – sat and listened to the speakers on the stage. The person at the microphone was Monty Taylor. He looked around the room. 'Progress comes through slow changes,' he began. 'I am here because these ladies …'

A door opened at the back of the room and several of the Dagenham women walked in.

Monty's smile disappeared for a moment.

'… these *lovely*, brave ladies,' he continued, 'are fighting for equal pay. But the unions must provide support for *all* its workers. Perhaps these ladies are asking for too much, too soon.'

Brenda had heard enough. 'Monty Taylor, you lied to us!' she shouted angrily from the back of the room. Other women were shouting too. Many of the union reps started to look around.

On stage, Monty called for quiet. 'We can talk about this ourselves later,' he said to the women.

But one of the reps stood up and said, 'Monty, I've seen more of these women in the newspapers in the last few weeks than you've managed in twenty years. I'd like to hear from them.'

Several people shouted their support. Monty looked unhappy, but he couldn't do anything to stop this now. As Rita walked towards the stage, he offered his hand to help her up the steps. Rita didn't take it – she didn't need Monty Taylor's help.

From the microphone, she looked out at all the faces in front of her. Everybody was waiting for her to speak. Rita thought about George's funeral and her fight with Eddie. Suddenly it was hard to find the words. She closed her eyes for a moment.

'My best friend just lost her husband,' she said at last. 'He was in the RAF* in the war. I asked him once why he joined the RAF and he said, "You've got to do something, haven't you?"' Rita looked around. 'You *had* to do something! Because it was *right*. If you didn't, how could you look at yourself in the mirror? When did that change? When did we stop fighting?'

The union reps were all silent now.

* *The RAF* = The Royal Air Force

'You've got to support us now. You've got to stand up with us.' Rita was speaking through her tears, but her voice was strong. 'We are the workers of this country – the men *and* the women. We need to fight, like our friend George, for what is right. And equal pay for women *is* right.'

❁ ❁ ❁

Later in the bar everybody was talking excitedly about Rita's speech. All of the Dagenham women were proud of her. But Rita was quiet. She turned and saw a nervous face at the doors. It was Eddie. Rita understood – after their fight that morning, Eddie had jumped on his motorbike and ridden all the way to Eastbourne.

She pushed past the people in the bar to see him. The two of them went outside.

'I … came to say sorry,' Eddie began. 'I … thought about what you said, and you were right. You *are* right!'

This wasn't easy for him. 'I'm proud of everything that you've done, Rita O'Grady, and I want to support you. I came to tell you that. But when I arrived, you were already on the stage and … you were amazing.' He smiled sadly. 'Maybe my support doesn't really matter to you, not now? Anyway, you get back to your meeting.' He turned away.

'Eddie?' Rita wasn't going anywhere. 'You've said some stupid things in your time, but …'

She ran to him and kissed him.

'Of course your support matters. It matters to me more than anything in the world!'

🌼 🌼 🌼

The union reps had voted. Had they decided to support the Dagenham women or not?

The speaker on the stage read out the results. 'The number of people who voted to support the Ford machinists: 79. The number against: 48.'

The women cheered. On stage Monty Taylor and Bartholomew looked away angrily. The Dagenham women had the support of all the unions.

CHAPTER 8
Making history

At Westminster, Barbara Castle had seen the conference report in the papers. She called her assistants to her office.

'I want to have a meeting with the Dagenham machinists,' she said. 'As soon as possible.'

The two men just stood there. They had worked with several top politicians before Mrs Castle. In their opinion, they knew more about how government worked than their new boss did.

'Ministers don't do things like that,' said one. 'Ever.'

'It will just give the strikers support,' added the other.

Mrs Castle gave them a long, hard look. 'Look at my hair,' she said. 'It's red and, like many people with red hair, I can become very angry.' She stood up calmly, then suddenly she shouted, 'Give them support? *Of course* they should have our support. They are striking for *equal pay*. If you two weren't so stupid, you would understand that!' She pointed at the two men. 'Go and set up a meeting now!'

The two assistants ran for the door.

✿ ✿ ✿

When Albert came round to Rita's flat, he found Eddie outside working on his motorbike. Rita was coming out with a cup of tea for her husband.

Albert's face was pale. 'What's wrong?' she asked.

Albert took Eddie's cup of tea. By the look of him, he needed it. 'Stay calm, Rita. I've just had a telephone call … from Barbara Castle's office. She wants you to come and meet her.'

Eddie looked up from the motorbike. 'What's happened now?' he asked.

'Barbara Castle wants to talk to me!' said Rita in disbelief. Eddie smiled proudly. 'Well done!'

❀ ❀ ❀

Peter Hopkins was looking out of his window when there was a knock at the door. He could not believe who was standing there – Rita O'Grady, the leader of the Dagenham women strikers! What was *she* doing at his house?

'It's OK,' Rita told him. 'I'm here to see your wife.'

Lisa joined her husband at the door. She knew that Peter was angry but she didn't care. 'Rita?' She gave a friendly smile. 'What are you doing here?'

Rita returned the smile. 'I need your help.'

Minutes later Rita left the house with Lisa's beautiful red dress. Now she was ready to go and meet a government Minister!

❀ ❀ ❀

There were reporters and photographers everywhere outside the government buildings in Westminster. They were shouting questions and taking photos as Rita, Brenda and Sandra pushed their way through. The other women cheered them from the street.

There was a line of policemen at the entrance to the buildings. Just as the three women went inside, somebody ran through the crowd and joined them. It was Connie!

'Sorry I'm late,' she said.

Rita took her friend's hands. The two women didn't need to say anything else.

The reporters were still shouting questions. 'What if Mrs Castle says no?' asked one. 'How will you go on?'

Rita gave him a hard look. 'How will we go on? We're *women*. Now don't ask such stupid questions.'

✿ ✿ ✿

Barbara Castle was ready to meet the Dagenham women, but somebody else had come to see her first. It was Bob Tooley from Ford.

'I wasn't expecting you,' she told him coolly. She knew how important Ford was to Britain, and she knew how important Tooley was at Ford.

'I hear you're meeting the Dagenham women,' he said.

Mrs Castle nodded. 'I think that it is time for me to hear their side of the story.' She started towards the door.

'I think that we both want the same thing, Mrs Castle,' said Tooley. 'To see Ford employing British workers.'

Mrs Castle turned. 'Ford is very important to this country, yes.'

'But if you can't help us to fight these strikes,' Tooley continued, 'we will take our factories somewhere else.'

Mrs Castle stepped back into the room. 'Are you trying to frighten me, Mr Tooley?' she said calmly.

'If you support the women, there's a chance that 40,000 Ford workers in this country may lose their jobs, Mrs Castle. I don't want to take that chance. And I don't think that you do either.'

✿ ✿ ✿

The four women from Dagenham sat in a waiting room. They looked around at the beautiful furniture and old paintings on the walls. They had come a long way from the machinists' area in the factory.

At last the office door opened and Mrs Castle walked in. The women were nervous, but Mrs Castle met them with a friendly smile. 'I know your face from the news, Mrs O'Grady,' she said.

'Call me Rita.'

When they were all sitting, Mrs Castle said, 'I fully support your fight for equal pay. And you will have it … but in time.'

'What?' asked Rita.

'Return to work,' continued Mrs Castle. 'Go back to your machines and I promise you this. This government will push forward with your fight.'

The polite smile had disappeared from Rita's face. 'No,' she said. 'We need something real, and we need it now. We thought that if we saw you ...'

Mrs Castle spoke straight to Rita. 'Sometimes politicians have to play a long game,' she began.

'We're not politicians,' said Rita quickly. 'We're working women ... and so are you.'

Mrs Castle gave a quick nod. She knew now that these women would not leave after just a friendly smile and a promise. 'What do you need to get back to work?' she asked. 'What is your 'something real'? And notice that I say *something*, not *everything* ...'

Rita thought quickly. 'We need ... to know that in the future we will get equal pay. And before that, we need to move much closer to the male rate of pay ... now, at Ford.'

'Seventy-five percent,' Mrs Castle offered.

Rita thought for a moment. 'Ninety,' she replied.

Mrs Castle looked at the other three women.

'Ninety,' Connie and Sandra agreed.

'At least,' added Brenda.

Mrs Castle continued to look right at Rita. 'You're putting me in a very difficult position,' she said.

✿ ✿ ✿

In another office, Bob Tooley was waiting. He was confident of the result. Ford was too big and too important. The British government didn't want to upset the company and lose so many jobs. As soon as the strikers were back at work, he could fly home to America.

The door opened. It was Mrs Castle.

'You know that chance that we were talking about, Mr Tooley?' she said. 'I'm going to have to take it.'

✿ ✿ ✿

Even more reporters and photographers waited outside to hear the result of Mrs Castle's meeting with the strikers. The other Dagenham women were waiting too.

On the other side of the gates, Mrs Castle and the four machinists waited to tell the world the news.

'I like your dress,' Mrs Castle said to Rita with a smile. 'I saw it in a magazine.'

Rita smiled. 'I have to give it back at the end of the day.'

The two women laughed together. Rita felt tired but happy. Finally two policemen pulled the heavy gates open. Mrs Castle stood to one side to let Rita go first.

'After you, young lady,' the Employment Minister said.

The four women held hands and they stepped out to face the world. Mrs Castle soon joined the women, putting her arms around them. She spoke to the reporters.

'I am happy to tell you that, after our talks this afternoon, the 187 Ford machinists will go back to work immediately. They will receive a pay rise which will put them at … ninety-two percent of the male rate.'

At first the crowd was quiet. Had they heard that correctly? Had the women really won?

'But that is not all,' continued Mrs Castle. 'As a result of our discussion, I can tell you that the government is in full support of a law for equal pay. Thank you!'

There was a huge cheer as the group of women strikers ran towards Rita. There were kisses, tears and smiles. They had won. The women of Dagenham had won their fight!

Two years later there was a new law in Britain: employers had to pay women and men the same rates for the same work. Similar laws followed in countries all around the world.

THE DAGENHAM STRIKE:
THE TRUE STORY

Made in Dagenham is based on the true story of the Ford machinists' strike in 1968. But who were the real women from Dagenham and what really happened?

The women in 2010

THE WOMEN

Before they started filming, the filmmakers spoke to some of the real Dagenham women.

Violet Dawson says that the strike 'frightened' Ford. This wasn't an easy time for her. Her husband did not support the strike.

Sheila Douglas lived at home with her parents and gave her weekly pay to her mum. Her parents supported the women's fight against the company.

Vera Sime worked while her sister looked after her children all day. 'We had half of the strike pay each,' Vera remembers.

There was no Rita O'Grady in real life. The character of Rita was based on a few different people. At one meeting with the management someone put some pieces of fabric on the table and asked the manager to put them together. But this was Bernie Passington. He was the union representative. In the film, the character Albert was based on him.

PAY GRADES

In 1967 new pay grades were introduced at Ford. The lowest was A (unskilled) and the highest was E (highly skilled). Each grade had a different rate of pay.

The machinists' job was grade B. All of the women knew that this was unfair. To get the job, they had to pass a test. At work they had to make over 30 seat covers every hour. It was difficult, dangerous work. Sheila Douglas says, 'We were fighting for the C grade at first. It became about equal pay later.'

After their meeting with Barbara Castle, the women went back to work on 92% of the male rate – but 92% of the male rate at grade B. Not all of the women were happy about this.

Some of the women outside Barbara Castle's office

EQUAL PAY

Employment Minister Barbara Castle helped to make a new law for equal pay in 1970. Under this law, women and men had to be paid the same rate for the same job.

But even with this and later laws, women have continued to receive less money at work. It is thought that even today women earn 82 pence for every pound that is earned by men in the UK.

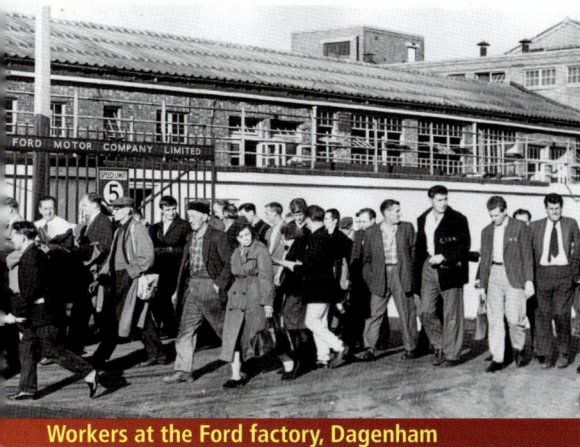

Workers at the Ford factory, Dagenham

Have there been any strikes in your country? What were the strikes about?

What do these words mean? You can use a dictionary.
based on   character
grade (n)

Women's lives

The 1960s were a time of great change in Britain. The strike in Dagenham was a sign of these changing times and an important moment in the history of women at work.

The world of work

At the start of the 1960s, most young women had a choice between having a career or getting married. Some married women – like many of the Dagenham machinists – had jobs, but they usually earned much less than the men. In most families, the husband was the person who earned most money.

Women and politics

Ideas were changing fast in the 1960s. People fought for rights for black people and they fought against the Vietnam War. The movement for equal rights for women was part of these changes in society.

Barbara Castle

Barbara Castle helped to make the workplace fairer for women with the law on equal pay (the Equal Pay Act). She was also one of the first successful female politicians in Britain. In 1964 she became a government minister for the first time.

Other countries – Ceylon (now Sri Lanka), India and Israel – had their first female political leaders in the 1960s. Britain did not have a woman Prime Minister until Margaret Thatcher in 1979.

Speaking against the Vietnam War, 1968

Women and marriage

One of the biggest changes in the 1960s came with the introduction of the birth control pill in 1961. Women had the chance to choose if and when they wanted to have children. This allowed more women to follow a career if they wanted.

There were other changes to life for married women. There was a new law in 1964 that half of any married couple's savings belonged to the woman.

How was life different for women in your country in the past?

Jean Shrimpton

Fashion

Even the fashions of the 1960s showed how women's lives were changing. In the 1950s women were expected to look and dress in a certain way. In 1965 model Jean Shrimpton shocked the country when she was photographed in a miniskirt. Soon lots of young women – like Sandra in *Made in Dagenham* – felt free to wear clothes like this, or any clothes that they wanted.

What do these words mean? You can use a dictionary.
career   birth control   savings   shock   miniskirt

Cars: an American dream

★

The first Ford car was built in America in the early 1900s. Since then cars have become the most popular form of transport in the world.

★ Henry Ford and the American Dream

Henry Ford started his company near the city of Detroit, in Michigan in the USA. His factories were the first to produce cars quickly and cheaply. This meant that many more people could buy cars. In 1908, Ford built the Model T and it became the most famous car in the world.

Henry Ford in the Model T

Cars became more and more important for American people. People believed that you weren't successful if you didn't have a car. The importance of the car helped to shape how towns and cities grew. Shopping areas in cities such as Los Angeles were built far from city centres because people could drive to them.

The first drive-in cinema opened in 1933. You could stay in your car to watch a movie. Today in the United States, you can buy dinner at a drive-in restaurant and visit a drive-in bank. In some places, you can even go to a drive-in church!

Watching a drive-in movie, 1949

Americans still love their cars, but the US is no longer the 'car capital' of the world.

★ In 2007 there were more than 500 cars for every 1,000 people in Germany Australia and Italy.

★ In 2010 a million more cars were made in China than in the United States.

At the Volkswagen company, Shanghai

★ **What colour?**

Henry Ford famously said that customers could have a Model T in any colour … if that colour was black! Today 24% of the world's cars are still black. The most popular colour for a car – 26% – is silver.

★ **What next?**

What will cars be like in the future? There are already cars that don't use petrol. In 2011 Ford introduced their first electric passenger car. We can't predict the popular cars of the future, but we can be almost certain one of them will be a Ford!

TOYOTA
一汽丰田与您相约E3
COROLLA 卡罗拉

★ **Did you know?**

The most successful family of cars is the Toyota Corolla. More than 32 million people have bought one of these small family cars.

★ What is your dream car?

What do these new words mean? You can use a dictionary.
transport   drive-in   predict

CHAPTERS 1–2

Before you read

1 Complete the sentences with these words.

cheer   complain   mark   overtime   rate   sewing   skilled   union

a) In our job we get more money when we work … .

b) If you aren't happy about something, you should … .

c) She has always liked … and makes all her own clothes.

d) Is it fair to give younger workers a lower … of pay?

e) There was a big … from the crowd when our team won.

f) He left a dirty … on the floor with his shoes.

g) The workers' … had meetings every month.

h) You need to do a course before you start the job. It is … work.

2 Match the words with the sentences.

fabric   horn   housing estate   nod   representative   strike

a) This makes a loud sound.

b) Clothes are made of this.

c) This person is chosen to speak for others.

d) This is when workers stop working because they want management to make changes.

e) An area where a lot of similar houses or flats are built.

f) To move your head up and down to say yes.

After you read

3 Answer the questions.

a) What do the women at the factory make?

b) Who is the factory's union rep?

c) Why has Albert already complained to the management?

d) Why does Rita's son have marks on his hand?

e) Why does Rita have pieces of fabric with her at the meeting?

f) After the meeting with management, what do the women at the factory do?

4 What do you think? What will the Ford management do about the women's strike?

CHAPTERS 3-5

Before you read

5 Match the words with their definitions. You can use a dictionary.
- **a)** support
- **b)** demand
- **c)** progress
- **d)** society
- **e)** equality

- **i)** having the same rights as others
- **ii)** ask strongly for something
- **iii)** people and how they live together
- **iv)** changes that make things better for people
- **v)** agree with and help

After you read

6 Put these sentences in the right order.
- **a)** The union men are angry with Albert.
- **b)** The women go on strike for twenty-four hours.
- **c)** American Bob Tooley arrives in the UK.
- **d)** Peter Hopkins tells Bob Tooley about the women's strike.
- **e)** The women decide to go on strike for a longer time.
- **f)** Women workers in other Ford factories join the strike.
- **g)** Ford decide to close the factory until the strike ends.
- **h)** The women go to Westminster.
- **i)** The management write a letter to the women.

7 Are these sentences about Rita true or false? Correct the false sentences.
- **a)** Monty tells Rita about his mother.
- **b)** Rita signs the letter about Mr Clarke.
- **c)** She tells the women to demand equal holidays.
- **d)** She is nervous about giving a speech in Liverpool.
- **e)** She is interviewed by a TV reporter.
- **f)** She is part of a political group.

8 Choose one of these people and write a page from their diary. Say what is happening at the Ford factory and what you think about it.
Bob Tooley   Lisa Hopkins   Albert   Barbara Castle

CHAPTERS 6–8

Before you read

9 Complete the sentences with these words.

conference   funeral   grave   stage

a) You can see the … from all parts of the theatre.

b) Most people came to the … to hear the political leader's speech.

c) My grandfather died last year. A lot of his old friends came to his … .

d) Since her husband died, my grandmother always leaves flowers next to his … .

10 What do you think? The strike is becoming more difficult for Rita. Will she continue her fight? Will she win? Why / Why not?

After you read

11 Who is speaking? Match the names with the sentences.

Connie   Mrs Castle   Eddie   Lisa Hopkins
Monty Taylor   Rita   Bob Tooley

a) 'Go and break this strike, please.'

b) 'Perhaps these ladies are asking for *too much*, *too soon*.'

c) 'We are the workers of this country – the men *and* the women.'

d) 'I've got to look after George. He only has me.'

e) 'Welcome to the real world, Rita.'

f) 'I loved reading about all these amazing people making history.'

g) 'This government will push forward with your fight.'

12 Answer the questions.

a) Why does Rita go to Eastbourne?

b) Why does Eddie follow her there?

c) Why does Rita borrow a dress from Lisa?

d) Why does Bob Tooley go to Westminster?

e) Why do the women agree to go back to work?

13 What do you think? Did the end of the story surprise you? Why did Barbara Castle support the Dagenham women?

14 Write adjectives to describe these characters.

Barbara Castle   Eddie   Rita   Bob Tooley